Right for Me

Written by Gill Munton

Illustrated by Ilaria Falorsi

OXFORD
UNIVERSITY PRESS

I am in the wood!
La la la ...

2

I can see a log cabin!
I will go in.

4

This dish is
no good!

This dish is
no good!

This is the right dish for me!

Ted

Mum

Dad

7

This chair is
no good!

This chair is
no good!

This is the right chair for me!

I will go into the bedroom.

This bed is
no good!

This bed is
no good!

This is the right
bed for me!

Zzzzz

Tum tee tum ...

Retell the story

Once upon a time...

The end.